THE CATCHER'S COMMAND

Mastering the Diamond

Behind the Plate

Skills, Strategies, and Leadership

SKY BENSON

Table of Contents

CHAPTER 1

THE CATCHER'S CRAFT

Developing strong receiving

"And framing skills"

All of the movements that a catcher makes behind the plate are like a quiet symphony. It is vital to note that every squat, shift, and glove movement communicates with the pitcher and, more significantly, influences the umpire's call. The art of accepting pitches and framing them is right at the center of this discourse that is taking place in silence. It is a quality that differentiates decent catchers from great catchers, allowing them to turn calls that are on the verge of becoming strikes into calls that are favorable to your pitcher. To transform yourself into a defensive maestro, here is how you can build good receiving and framing skills:

Establishing the Groundwork: The Fundamentals of Glovework

Before becoming a wizard of framing, you must have a rock-solid basis for receiving. The first step is to ensure that the glove fits snugly and comfortably. The glove you wear should have the sensation of being an extension of your hand, enabling you to make smooth catches without compromising your control. You should practice fundamental receiving drills with a partner or a coach, primarily focusing on catching pitches at different spots within the zone. Maintain a strong and stable focus for the pitcher while holding your glove below your chest and angling toward the umpire. This will help you achieve your goal. Acquiring a command of the mitt is essential. Get used to making a smooth transition from your catching hand to your throwing hand rapidly and silently. Doing so reduces the amount of wasted movement and ensures you are prepared to shoot the ball down to any base. Maintaining clean catches and a smooth transfer should be your priority as a catcher because dropped balls are the cardinal sin.

Understanding the Art of Framing and How to Direct the Umpire's Eye

The fun portion, which is now framed, has arrived! Through the subtle manipulation of your glove, you can create the illusion that a pitch is closer to the strike zone than it is. This technique is known as framing. To perform this delicate dance, you need to have a firm grasp of the strike zone and the ability to respond swiftly to pitches that are coming in.

Some critical approaches for framing

The "Catch Down" technique tells you to angle your glove slightly downwards when you catch the ball while catching low pitches in the zone. Doing so creates the impression that the pitch came close to touching the bottom of the strike zone. The "Up and In" technique involves turning your glove slightly inwards when you grab the ball to catch pitches on the inside half of the plate. This moves the ball closer to the area that is considered to be the strike zone. The "High Steal" When pitching at pitches on the verge of being high, you should keep your glove firm and avoid raising it too much. It is possible to make a high pitch appear almost catchable by using a relaxed glove with the ball tucked deep inside.

Exercising shadow framing drills is a great way to improve your skills.

The development of your framing instincts requires that you devote yourself and practice. The practice of shadow framing comes into play at this point. Consider the possibility of pitches coming in from various directions while you are in your catching position. Imitate the appropriate framing approach for each pitch, concentrating on small motions that allow you to achieve the greatest possible illusion. This prepares your muscle memory and reaction time for circumstances you will encounter in the game.

Develop Your Skills as a Student of the Game

Listen to replays of Major League Baseball catchers famous for their framing talents. Examine the movements of their gloves and the subtle ways in which they control the ball while it is on the edge of the zone. Attend to how they arrange themselves for the various pitches and adjust their framing following this. Regarding your technique, you should seek advice and criticism from your coach or a catcher with more experience.

Developing a Relationship of Compatibility with Your Pitching Staff

Great framing is not something that occurs in a vacuum. The importance of trust and communication with your pitchers cannot be overstated. The most excellent way to frame them for strikes is to discuss their preferred spots for pitches and how you can best frame them. Collaborate with them during bullpen sessions to acquire their hallmark pitches and establish a mutual comprehension of how to make the most of their efficacy.

Review of the Video: Some Analysis and Refinement

Game film is your most trusted companion. Your performance behind the plate should be evaluated, with a particular emphasis on your receiving and framing techniques. Determine areas to improve and try various methods to present the problem. This self-analysis lets you improve your technique and become a well-rounded defensive player.

Framing is an art form and not a science. Umpires are human beings susceptible to being swayed by a pitch that is presented appealingly. Nevertheless, maintain your morality. When trying to improve the perceived position of a tight pitch, it is essential to avoid overt manipulation and instead concentrate on subtle motions. You can transform yourself from a passive receiver into an active game-changer behind the plate if you rigorously practice these methods. Through these practices, you will strengthen the skills of receiving and framing. It is possible for a well-framed pitch to make the difference between a strikeout and a base runner, making it possible for your team to change the momentum of the game in their favor. To begin mastering the art of receiving and framing, you should put on your glove, go behind the plate, and begin the process!

Mastering the art

"Of blocking pitches."

You're not just the game's director, calling pitches and telling your pitcher how to hit the ball. You're also the last line of defense, a brick wall between a fastball that goes too far and you or a friend who doesn't see it going to the hospital. It is essential for a catcher who wants to do well behind the plate to learn how to block pitches. Here's a detailed look at how to change yourself from an easy target to an unstoppable force:

Building a Fortress: The Right Gear and How to Stand

Having the right gear is the first step to good blocking. Spend your money on a good chest protector that can absorb pressure and let you move freely. It's also essential to have a catcher's mitt that fits well, has good padding, and a safe thumb guard. Let's talk about stance now. Stand with your feet shoulder-width apart to make a stable base and your knees slightly bent. Drop your hips a little to lower your center of gravity. You can handle the ball's force in this balanced position while staying in control behind the plate.

Target Acquisition: Don't Lose Your Eye on the Ball

Blocking is all about what to do and how to respond. Keep your eyes on the pitcher's hand the whole time they throw. You can change your position and glove angle by observing the ball's path after it leaves your hand. Don't peek at the hitter or guess where the pitch will land. Without a doubt, your eyes are on the ball.

Basics of Glovework: Making a Shield

Your hand is the main thing you use to block. Hold your glove below chest level as the pitch gets closer and make a big target. You can pocket the ball by angling the hand toward your body. Don't forget that a more significant object is more accessible to catch. Don't try to catch every pitch that is stopped. There are times when misdirection is very helpful. When the ball is coming at you fast, try to steer it away from you and into the ground. A well-placed deflection can keep a wild pitch from hitting the catcher or hurting someone on the team.

Getting good at different blocking moves

There isn't a single way to block that works for everyone. For each pitch, you need a different set of techniques:

Fastballs: For these high-heat balls, use your glove to hit a big target and keep your arm strong so it can handle the impact. To help take the force, lean back and spread your body weight. Regarding breaking balls, sliders and curveballs tend to move more and can dart in surprising directions. Keep your balance and be ready to change the angle of your glove at the last second to block the ball.

Changes: These slower pitches can be hard to block because of how fast they seem. Focus on being quick to respond and deflecting them into the ground as much as possible to keep them from bouncing away.

Building Strength and Conditioning: A Powerhouse Catcher

Blocking isn't just about skill; you also need to be solid and able to keep going for a long time. Work on your core power to keep your base stable and absorb impact. You need strong legs for quick side-to-side movement and recovery after stopping a pitch. Squats, lunges, and core work should all be part of your workout routine.

Practice makes perfect: drills to get better at what you do

Getting good at blocking takes time and effort, just like with any other skill. Here are some excellent drills that will help you get better at blocking:

Partner drills: Have a friend throw tennis or soft practice balls from far away and in different places. Get better at blocking and sending the ball into the dirt with your hand.

The "Bullpen Sessions": Focus on blocking drills when you work with your pitchers in the field. Ask them to throw breaking balls and fastballs low in the zone to make it feel like wild pitches you might see in a game.

Mirror Drills: In front of a mirror, act out different blocking pitches from various angles. This helps you get faster at reacting and get better at glovework.

Building Mental Toughness

To be good at blocking, you need to be mentally tough. Do not be scared of the ball! Be sure of yourself and stand tall behind the plate. Take on the task and picture yourself blocking every pitch perfectly. A block that works better is not afraid of anything.

Talking to your pitcher is very important.

To block well, you need to be able to talk to your pitcher. Talk about the pitches they can make and the ones that might "get away" from them. This lets you guess what wild pitches might happen and set yourself up for them.

Review of the video: Looking at how you block

Look at the game film to figure out how you're stopping. Were you quick enough to act? Was your glove in the right place? Find things that could be done better and try different real-life stopping methods. Stopping is not the same as being a human shield. It's about deflection that you can control and keep yourself and your friends from getting hurt. You can become a confident backstop who makes pitchers trust you by putting proper equipment, body positioning, and response time at the top of your priorities.

Higher Level Techniques

For this move, you put one knee on the ground on the side where you think the ball will miss. This gives you a smaller target and lets you change directions faster, but you must be flexible and quick. To do this, get on all fours and hold your glove low and at an angle to the inside. It protects your body as much as possible but makes it harder to move around. This method should only be the last option for crazy pitches.

How to Stay Sharp

Do movement and stretching exercises regularly to ensure you can move quickly and respond to pitches that come out of the blue. Do specific blocking drills before every game to rapidly prepare your body and reflexes.

Attitude on Game Day

During the game, stay in the present moment. Don't think about a block you missed in the past or worry about one that might come up. Focus on how you naturally respond to each pitch. If a pitch hits the corner of your glove but is still called a ball, tell the judge what you think in a calm voice. A polite answer can sometimes tip the scales in your favor in a close case.

Becoming a great blocker takes time, hard work, and a desire to learn from mistakes. In the short term, the pain of missing a block might push you. Still, your long-term goal should be to become reliable and safe. You'll go from being a passive target to an aggressive guardian behind the plate by repeatedly working on your blocking skills. This will earn your pitcher's respect and strengthen your team's defense.

Perfecting your throwing

"To second and third bases."

As a catcher, you're not just the base of the defense behind home plate. You're also a quiet killer and a powerful thrower when stopping runners on base. A strong arm and a quick release can turn an attempt to steal a base into a booming out, which can change the course of the game in your favor. Here are some tips on how to get better at throwing to second and third base and become a throwing machine:

Footwork and mechanics are part of "Building the Foundation."

The first step to a good throwing move is having good footwork. Quickly and easily get the ball in your hand. It is imperative that you can easily switch from using your catching hand to your throwing hand. When saves are lost, valuable seconds are lost. As you move the ball from one hand to the other, plant your back foot firmly in the direction of your throw with a decisive step. This makes a stable base for producing electricity. When you throw, put your front foot forward and fall slightly close to second or third base. This gives you speed and helps you turn your hips for a strong throw. Finish your throw with a strong follow-through after you let go of the ball. This ensures precision and speeds things up the most.

Mastering the mechanics of throwing

You need more muscular arms to throw things. It's about making power by using processes that work well. Get a good grip on the ball so you can easily throw it. You can control and aim the ball well with a four-seam grip, and your throws will sink with a two-seam hold. To make power, use your whole body, not just your arm. As you throw, turn your hips and torso toward the goal. This will give the ball more power. Keep your throwing arm tight and close to your body during the whole move. When your arm is extended and loops around, it can make you less accurate and weak. When you let go of the ball, snap your wrist to give it more speed. Picture moving your wrist back and forth like a slingshot.

Build a throwing machine to work on your strength and conditioning.

It takes time to get better at throwing. Here are some exercises that will make your throwing arm stronger and help you throw better overall:

Long Toss: Do long toss drills as part of your regular training practice. Over time, slowly extend the distance, focusing on throwing mechanics and accuracy before aiming for the highest speed.

Weighted Ball Work: Throwing weighted balls short distances can help your throwing muscles get stronger. Remember that good skills are more important than brute force.

Plyometric Exercises: Box jumps and squats are two exercises that help build explosive strength, which makes throwing faster.

Strengthening the Core: A strong core keeps you stable and helps your lower body send power to your throwing arm.

Getting Better at Throwing

A strong arm is useless if you can't aim with great accuracy. Throw against a wall or net that has targets marked on it. This helps you get better at regularly hitting certain spots. Have a partner play second and third base to act like baserunners. This will help you work on your throwing accuracy in a way that feels like a real game. Picture yourself throwing the ball to second and third base successfully. This thought practice helps you concentrate and boosts your confidence in throwing skills.

"Game Day Mentality: Staying Sharp and Calm"

You must pay attention to something else to throw well during a game. Look at the situation and be ready for theft attempts. As the pitcher throws, pay attention to the baserunner's body language and how they move. Talk to your pitcher and infielders about possible steal efforts. This lets everyone know what's going on and act quickly. Don't let stress affect you. Keep your cool when things get tough. Keeping cool helps you use the proper technique to make a good throw.

Advanced Throwing Skills

You hop slightly off the ground after passing the ball for this move. This gives your throw more speed and power. It takes time and a good balance to get good at it. Do quick-release drills to reduce the time to catch and throw the ball. That little extra time can mean the difference between an out and a stolen base.

Looking at how you throw

Take a video of yourself throwing during games or practice. Watch the video again to look at your movement, how you throw, and how you follow through. Find things that could be done better and try different methods. It takes time and hard work to throw correctly and quickly. Don't give up if you don't see effects right away. You can go from being a shaky thrower to a reliable weapon behind the plate with consistent practice, patience, and a focus on proper techniques. Here are some more things to think about:

How to Stay Healthy

Take the time to do a good warm-up routine before games or throwing drills. Light jogging, dynamic stretches, and arm circles are some exercises that will prepare your body for throwing. Give your arm enough time to rest between throwing lessons to keep it from getting hurt from overuse. Pay attention to your body and rest when you need to. Do flexibility exercises regularly as part of your routine to keep your arms loose and mobile, which can affect how you throw.

Getting the Most Out of Each Throw

Know how to play different outfield positions based on the runner on base, the situation, and the pitch type. For example, if a fast runner is at second base, you might choose a faster throw over a more accurate one. Learn how to throw in a way that looks like you're not throwing, especially when trying to catch a steal.

A quick secret throw can catch the runner on base off guard, which increases your chances of getting them out. Work on short throws and backup plays with your infielders. This ensures the ball is caught neatly, even if your throw isn't perfect. This stops mistakes and records them.

Mental Strength

Don't let a lousy throw define you. Everybody messes up sometimes. Take what you learned from them, change how you do things, and try again. Trust that you can make the throw. A positive attitude leads to a smoother throwing motion and better aim. As the catcher, you're in charge of defense and the game from behind home plate. Enjoy the stress of catching base stealers and the thrill of stopping the other team's offense.

You'll go from being a passive receiver to a dynamic force behind the plate if you keep working on these skills and build a well-rounded approach. To throw well, you need more than just a strong arm. To become a real throwing machine and a defensive powerhouse, you need to know a lot about the game, be able to talk to your teammates clearly, and keep your mind focused at all times. Take your ball and go to the field to work on your throws! The game waits for you to be great at bat.

CHAPTER 2

CONTROLLING THE GAME

Calling a smart

"And strategic game"

As a catcher, you're not just a wall for defense or a machine for throwing. Behind the plate, you're the orchestra's director. Mastering the art of calling pitches can make the difference between struggling batters and pitchers getting upset, affecting the game's outcome. Here are some tips that will help you go from being a passive receiver to an intelligent mastermind:

Know Your Arsenal: Weak and Strong Points of the Pitcher

Calling an intelligent game starts with deep knowledge of your pitcher's repertoire. Have an in-depth talk with your starter before every match. Talk about what they're good at: is it a hot fastball, a sneaky curveball, or a nasty changeup? It's also important to know what their flaws are. For example, do they have trouble controlling a specific pitch or get stuck in a particular spot? This information will be your tool. You want to show off your pitcher's good qualities and downplay their bad ones. A call pitch that highlights their best features and stays away from areas where they are more likely to get struck.

Scouting the Enemy: Looking at the Hitter

It's essential to know your pitcher, but it's also necessary to understand the other team's players. Scouting reports before a game become your guide. Look at how the batter usually hits. Does he sit on fastballs or have trouble with breaking balls? Does he pull everything or know how to use two strikes well? This study lets you guess how he will act and make calls that reflect his weaknesses. For instance, if you're facing a fastball hitter, you might start by breaking balls to throw him off, then sneaking a fastball by him later in the count.

An orchestra of pitches called "The Art of Sequencing."

When you call pitches, you don't just throw your pitcher's whole collection at them. It's about putting together a sequence, a story told in different voices. The fastball is what most pitchers do for a living. Start most of the batters' turns with a fastball to make them remember it. Later, off-speed pitches will be more misleading because of this. Don't be afraid to switch between places. Ask batters to hit hard with high fastballs, low-breaking balls, and away pitches. Ask batters to hit for strikes outside the strike zone with low-breaking balls. Make the batter guess, and then guess wrong. If a batter sees fastballs all night, they also don't work. Add curveballs, sliders, and changeups to your off-speed pitches to mess up the batter's timing and keep him off balance.

Reading the Situation: Making Changes Right Away

In baseball, even the best-laid plans often go wrong. A batter could change how he hits in the middle of an at-bat, or your pitcher could lose control of a particular pitch. You must be able to change:

Reading the Swing: Pay close attention to how the batter swings the bat. Is he going to break balls? If so, throw him more fastballs to take advantage of his anger.

Pitcher Feel: Get to know your pitcher like a sixth sense. If they ignore your sign, which is a physical cue that the pitch is coming, talk to them about it. They might feel good about a pitch that wasn't your first call.

Count Baseball: How many balls and strikes are there? This tells you how to act. At first, you can challenge batters with strikes. When there are two strikes, getting them to ground out becomes more important.

A Group Project on the Art of Communication

You can't call pitches by yourself. You must talk to your player. Use a set of signs, like finger or small body movements, to send the sound selection without drawing attention to yourself. Talk about these signs before the game and stay consistent during it. It's essential to get along with your starter. Listen to what they say, and if they aren't sure about your call, talk about other options. Don't forget that you're working as a team to stop the other side.

"Getting Good at the Game" Situations:

It is essential to know how to call a game in different situations:

Bases Loaded: When there is a lot of pressure, and the bases are total, pitches that cause weak contact or groundouts should be given the most attention. The main goal is to limit damage as much as possible. There are two outs, and the runner is in scoring position. When men are on base, pitches that get them out are more important. Pay attention to fastballs that land well or breaking balls that cause pop-ups or strikes.

Total Count: When there is a complete count, things are tense. Use the batter's past habits and what you think will make him swing and miss to decide what pitch to throw. This is why it's important to know what his weakness is.

The Mental Game: How to Stay Calm and Cool

It takes a sharp mind and unwavering attention to call a good game. Everyone makes bad decisions. Take what you learned from them, change how you do things, and make your next pitch. Don't let a call you made in the past affect your choice now. Have faith in your pitcher's ability to do what you tell them to do. Players need to feel confident; they do better when you believe in them. Keep your cool when things get tough. When you're feeling upset, you make bad decisions. Take a deep breath, pay attention to what's happening, and confidently call the next pitch.

Using modern tools for technology and data

The game of today uses technology. Use tools like pitch data analysis to determine what your batters are destructive at and what your pitchers tend to do. Heatmaps can show you where certain pitches are most likely to be, so you can ask for pitches outside of those places to limit the damage. Don't forget that data is just a tool and not the law. Along with facts, use your gut feelings and ability to read games to make intelligent choices.

How to improve your game-calling.

Keep a record of yourself calling pitches during scrimmages or practice games. Afterward, watch the video again and think about the sequences you chose, the pitches you used in different situations, and how you talked to the player. Find ways to improve things and try new strategies in future games.

Learning More About Games

A good game caller keeps learning new things. Look at how experienced catchers call pitches, figure out how they work, and take notes on their methods. Talk to past players or coaches. Learn from their mistakes and gain helpful information about how to call the game. Delve deeply into game-calling resources and use different approaches and ideas.

It takes time, practice, and a constant desire to learn to become a great game caller. The best callers change, grow, and adapt as their jobs continue. You can go from being a passive receiver to a strategic mastermind behind the plate by constantly working on your skills, analyzing situations, and building a solid relationship with your pitcher. This will allow you to control the game's flow and ultimately lead your team to win. Get your gear together, learn how to play, and soon, you'll be the chess master who calls the shots from behind the plate!

Working effectively

"With your pitching staff"

There are other people with you as a catcher besides the person behind the plate. You two work well together, which is essential for good throwing staff. Your relationship with your pitchers, sometimes called the "battery," is significant to their success and, in the end, to your team's wins. Here are some tips on how to build trust, improve communication, and become a partner that your pitchers can count on:

Getting to Know Your Pitchers: Personalities, Weaknesses, and Strengths

You must know your pitchers personally and professionally to build a good battery. This is more than just remembering how fast their fastball is. Learn about them: Figure out which shots each pitcher does best. Is it a fastball that burns, a changeup that tricks you, or a sharp curveball that makes knees buckle? Let's talk about weaknesses. Everyone has them. Find out what pitches they have trouble handling or what parts of the zone they struggle with. Some pitchers are tough old pros, while others are young guns full of energy. Change the way you talk to them to fit their personalities. With this information, you can change how you pitch to each player. If the newbie is nervous, you might need to give them more encouragement and direction. A seasoned player might like a more collaborative method where you all talk about which pitches to use.

Mastering Communication: A Symphony of Silence

Catchers and pitchers talk to each other like a dance of signs and hints. Create a clear and consistent set of signs that you can use to show the pitch choice quietly. You can use finger movements or body language. Your signs must be clear, but it's hard for the hitter to read them. A thorough talk with your starting pitcher should happen before every game. Talk about the game plan, the hitting styles of the other team, and any specific areas they want to work on. Sometimes, you need to make a quick trip to the mound. You can use this time to support them, talk about making changes to the plan, or calm them down. Keep these meetings short and to the point to keep the game moving.

Getting people to trust and believe in you takes work on both ends.

A strong battery is built on trust and faith. When a catcher frames pitches for strikes and blocks wild pitches, the pitcher starts to trust them. Really and truly, they know you have their back. Even after a bad inning, show your players that you still believe in them. Being positive can help them feel better and get back on track with just a few words of support. When you're calling the game, let your pitchers make ideas. In some situations, they might feel safe throwing a particular pitch. Listen to what they say and think about what they must say as a group.

How to Deal with Setbacks: Mistakes as Learning Tools

Mess-ups happen a lot in baseball. There will be walks, hits, and even saves that are lost. You are to blame if you call a terrible pitch, and the ball hits it. It's OK to apologize and return to work on the next pitch immediately. Talk about a harrowing trip together after it's over. Figure out what went wrong and discuss how you can do better next time as a team. Don't let a lousy game turn into a bad day. Keep a good attitude and pay attention to the present. Tell your pitcher to do the same.

How to Become a Leader: A Guide

It's not enough to be a catcher; you have to be a leader on the field. Teach younger players what you know and use your own experience. Help them prepare for the game, give them tips on pitch choices, and improve their skills. Teach your pitchers how important it is to work hard, be dedicated, and have a good mood. Your hard work and dedication to the field will motivate them. Even though you should be helpful, don't be afraid to hold your pitchers responsible. It can help to be gently reminded to concentrate or to talk about physics.

Getting Better at Chemistry: Making a Bond

A strong generator does well away from the field, too. Plan team dinners or trips to get to know your pitchers outside of baseball and build friendships. Learn Their Interests. Show interest in their lives outside of baseball. What are their favorite things to do? A slight personal touch can go a long way. Celebrate wins with each other, huge ones. This emphasizes the benefits of working together as a team.

Looking at Your Speech

Record yourself while you play scrimmages or practice games. Afterward, watch the video again and pay attention to how you communicated. Were your signs clear? Did you offer quick support when you visited the mound? Did the player respond to what you said? Find ways to get better and try different ways of talking to people in future encounters.

Keeping Your Mind Sharp: Getting Ready for Different Personalities

As you work with different pitchers, be ready to change how you talk to them. A more emotional pitcher might need to be reassured constantly, while a more analytical pitcher might like to use facts to make decisions. Improve your emotional intelligence so that you can connect with each pitcher in a way that fits their personality.

Embrace how unpredictable the game is

Baseball is a game where things are constantly changing. In the middle of the game, a pitcher could lose control of their fastball, or a batter could suddenly start hitting breaking balls. If the other team is taking down your first signs, have extra signs ready to go up. Don't be afraid to whisper with your pitcher during the inning. Use subtle hand signs to change the location or type of pitch depending on the situation. Staying flexible means being ready to call off your pregame plan if needed. Having faith in your gut and calling strikes that you think will get out is sometimes the best thing to do.

It takes time, hard work, and a genuine desire to see your pitchers succeed in building a good battery. By building confidence, communication, and a good working relationship, you can go from being a catcher to an important teammate, the backbone of your pitching staff, and a significant factor in your team's wins. Put on your hat and call it a great game. Be the boss your pitchers can count on and off the field.

Hitter tendencies

"And exploiting weaknesses."

There are more things you can do as a catcher than play defense or call the ball. You're a detective trying to figure out the baseball code and exploit your opponent's flaws. If you know how batters approach the plate, you can work with your pitcher to make a series of pitches that trick batters into striking out or grounding. Here are some tips that will help you go from being a passive observer to a great strategist:

This is your secret weapon: "The Scouting Report."

The scouting report is your first line of defense. It has a lot of helpful information about the other team's players. Does the batter stand tall and block hard, or are they hunched over and waiting? Would he like to swing early in the count or wait for a pitch? Does he have a smooth, level swing or a strong uppercut? This could mean that they like fastballs or breaking balls. These are the places where the batter hits the ball most often. Does he hit the ball hard enough to pull it to the outside of the plate, or can he have good gap power and hit it anywhere? When it comes to splits, how does the batter do against left-handed, right-handed, fastball, and breaking ball pitchers? Read the scouting report over and over again. Before every game, you should carefully read it and look for patterns and trends in how each batter hits the ball. This knowledge is what your game plan is built on.

Reading Body Language: Cutting Through the Noise

A sharp eye is constructive for figuring out how a batter hits. A batter who wags his bat quickly might try to swing early in the count, especially if the pitch is fast. A small change in stance could show a preference for a particular spot. For example, moving toward the plate could mean a fastball choice, while a leg kick could mean getting ready for a breaking ball. The way a batter looks can give you a hint. If you look high in the zone, you might be prepared for a fastball; if you look low, you might be ready for a breaking ball. Don't forget that these are only signs and not promises. Hitting experts are very good at hiding their tells, but these minor signs tell a lot about how they will hit.

Taking Advantage of Weaknesses: Customizing Your Approach

It's time to plan to use a hitter's weaknesses once you know what they are. If you're facing a fastball bat, you should start with breaking balls to throw them off. As the count goes on, sneak a fastball by them when they expect another slow pitch. Using fastballs in various places, like high, low, and away, can worsen their timing. If you have a batter who has trouble with off-speed pitches, work fastballs early and often to make them a part of your game. Breaking balls should be thrown at every batter. Focus on sharp curves or sliders that leave the strike zone and make the batter chase. When facing a pull hitter, you should throw pitches on the outside half of the plate. This will make them reach for pitches out of their comfort zone. Pull-hit people tend to be late on fastballs and might swing and miss on a slower pitch so that changeups can be very useful against them.

Changing Things on the Spot: The Unexpected

Even the best-planned plans can go wrong. Batters may change how they hit during the at-bat, or your pitcher may lose control of a particular throw. After each pitch, watch how the batter swings the bat. Is he going to break balls? If so, pay attention to fastballs. Get to know your pitcher like a sixth sense. Talk about it if they ignore your sign, which is a wordless message about the pitch choice. They might feel good about a pitch that wasn't your first call. How many balls and strikes are there? This tells you how to act. As early as possible, you can throw strikes at batters. When there are two strikes, getting the ground out becomes essential.

A Tricky Dance: The Art of Sequencing

When you call pitches, you don't just throw your pitcher's whole collection at them. It's about putting together a series of pitches that trick the batter and keep them thinking. The fastball is what most pitchers do for a living. Start most of the batters' turns with a fastball to make them remember it. Later, off-speed pitches will be more misleading because of this. Don't be afraid to switch between places. Ask batters to hit hard with high fastballs, low-breaking balls, and away pitches. Ask batters to hit for strikes outside the strike zone with low-breaking balls. Make the batter guess, and then guess wrong. If a batter sees fastballs all night, they also don't work. Add curveballs, sliders, and changeups to your off-speed pitches to mess up the batter's timing and keep him off balance.

The Second Guess for Anticipating Changes

Hitters who are innovative change how they hit throughout the game. A batter will be more choosy when they face your pitcher for the second time in a game. They might be sitting on a particular pitch based on what they saw earlier. Switch up the order, make pitches they expect, and keep them thinking. When there is a complete count, things get tough. You should call a pitch based on how the batter usually hits and what you think will make him swing and miss. This is where knowing his weakness is fundamental. If it's hard for him to break balls down in the zone, throw him a sharp curveball for a strike three.

Using Modern Tools: How to Get the Most Out of Technology

The game of today uses technology. Use tools like pitch data analysis to determine what your batters are destructive at and what your pitchers tend to do. Heatmaps can show you where certain pitches are most likely to be, so you can ask for pitches outside of those places to limit the damage. Do not forget that data is not a master but a tool. Along with facts, use your gut feelings and ability to read games to make intelligent choices.

Looking at Your Pitch Choice

Keep a record of yourself calling pitches during scrimmages or practice games. Afterward, watch the video again and pay attention to which pitches you used for which batters. Did you take advantage of their weaknesses well? Did you change how you were hitting as the at-bat went on? Figure out what you must work on and try new strategies against similar players in the next game.

Learning for Life: An Ongoing Journey

A good catcher who knows how to handle batters is constantly learning to watch Major League Baseball Games and pay attention to how experienced catchers call pitches for different batters. Look at how they're putting things together and their methods. Ask past players or coaches for advice. Find out what kinds of hitting patterns they've seen and how they change how they stand behind the plate. Learn as much as you can about how hitters usually play and how to use different strategies in your game plan.

If you want to get good at knowing hitters, you have to work at it. The best catches watch, think about, and change all the time. When you use these tactics, you'll go from being a passive observer to a master strategist who can determine how the other team hits, take advantage of their weaknesses, and win the game. Get your gear together, learn the game, and become the catcher that makes batters scratch their heads as they walk back To the bench.

CHAPTER 3

OFFENSIVE CONTRIBUTIONS

Hitting for power

"And consistency"

Every batter dreams of hearing the crack of the bat, hearing the crowd roar, and seeing the ball fly out of the stadium. But you need more than raw strength to get power and accuracy at the plate. A lot of practice, timing, and movements go into it. Here's how to become a powerful but accurate hitter that people fear:

Mechanics are essential for building a solid foundation.

Power-hitting is based on having a smooth, efficient move. This is called "stance," and it sets the tone for everything that comes next. Keep your feet shoulder-width apart and your knees slightly bent. This will help you stay comfortable and steady. It's essential to have a firm grip on the bat that doesn't hurt. Find a grip that lets you keep control of the bat while you swing it without getting tense. The action that coils the bat before the swing stores potential energy that can be released later. This is called the bat load. Keep your weight back on your heels and hands during this time.

The Power Stroke: Let the Kraken Free

Your hips are where your power is. Think of them spinning quickly toward the pitcher. That energy will flow through your belly and into your swing. Try not to spin or chop the ball. For the most strength, swing the bat level so that the ball hits the bat's sweet spot. Don't stop once you hit it off. When you finish your swing with your front foot pointed at the pitcher, that's a strong follow-through. This makes sure that all of your power goes into the ball.

The "sweet spot" of success is when you find the right time.

Power doesn't mean anything without time. Pay attention to when the pitcher lets go of the ball and follows it as it leaves their hand. This helps you guess when the pitch will come and adjust your swing correctly. Time management is harmed by stress. Let go of your upper body and concentrate on a smooth, steady swing. Allow your body to respond quickly to the pitch. The ability to hit is short-lived. It will get easier to time pitches as you see live ones in batting practice or practice games.

Getting Consistent

You can focus on throws you can hit if you know what a strike is and what it's not. You need to be disciplined at the plate to avoid bad swings and improve your chances of getting a good pitch. "Go into every at-bat with a plan." Do you want to hit a home run or try to get the ball into play? A clear plan for what to do will help you choose which pitches to hit. You have to think about things when you play baseball. Learn how to stay focused, get out of a slump, and get back on track after a strikeout. Your secret weapon is in a good mood.

Strength training and conditioning: putting together a substantial body

Working out your core is essential to move power from your legs to your swing. Do movements that work your lower back, obliques, and abs. Exercises that build rotational power, like medicine ball throws and weighted bat swings, can help you make your swing more torque-based. Being balanced and flexible makes it easier to use your power and keeps you from getting hurt. As part of your routine, do some stretching and balance routines.

"Learn from the Best: Examine and Change"

The greats didn't get that way overnight. Pay close attention to how good hitters move and hit the ball. Watch how they change their swing depending on the ball and the situation. Get hitting tips from teachers with a lot of experience or sign up for hitting clinics. These can give you helpful information and tailored comments. Take a video of yourself hitting and look at it later. Find places to improve and try different drills to help you do that. Getting more robust and more consistent is a process, not a goal. Remember to be patient, persistent, and committed to your work. An intelligent approach, better timing, and fine-tuning your movements will help you become the feared hitter you dream of being.

Getting Hit on Different Types of Pitches

If you make fastballs, they'll be your primary source of income. To throw a high fastball, keep your swing level and on top of the pitch. For a line drive or a low fastball, move your body slightly in the swing to get under the ball and hit it on the ground. These leave the strike zone as they get close to the plate. Before you swing, be calm and wait for the curve to break. Going for home runs with a level swing and a slight uppercut is possible. These are slower than fastballs and are meant to trick you. Pay attention to spotting the changeup early and slowing your swing to hit the ball hard.

Hitting All Fields

Don't only hit home runs to right field when you pull the bat. Gain the skill to hit the ball anywhere on the field: Learn how to hit line drives between the outfielders to get doubles and triples. You need to be able to handle your bat well and change your swing depending on where the pitch is coming from. A well-placed ground ball can sometimes be more beneficial than a big home run. In critical cases, learn how to change your swing so that you hit the ball on the ground for RBIs.

Taking Care of Your Body

Feed your body the right foods to get the most out of your workouts. Pay attention to healthy fats, complicated carbs, and lean protein. Your body needs time to get back to normal after hitting. Make sure you get enough sleep and take breaks during your workouts. Pay attention to your body, and don't do things that hurt you. The proper warm-up and cool-down exercises can help keep you from getting hurt.

Becoming a great player takes time, hard work, and a game love.
Everything will go up and down, work well, and not work well. Remember
what you've learned, stay upbeat, and have fun. I'll never get
tired of hitting a baseball.

Utilizing situational hitting

"And smart base running."

It's not all about hitting substantial home runs or getting hitters out with fastballs that are too fast. You must plan your moves because every out and every base hit can change the result. This is where hitting for power and running smart come in handy. These things turn you from a good baseball player into a genius who sees the bigger picture and uses their skills to help their team win.

Thoughts Beyond Homer on Situational Hitting

It's not about hitting hard; it's about making intelligent choices at the plate based on what's going on. It's time to step up! When someone is on second or third base, it's your job to get them home. You should try to hit ground balls or line drives that get past the infield, even if it means giving up speed. A well-placed single can bring in runs just as well as a home run. Your goal might be to move the runner from first base to second base early in the game when there are no outs or only one out. A bunt, a ground ball to the right side, or a well-placed fly ball can put the runner in a scoring position and give the next player a chance to score an RBI. A sacrifice fly could be the best move if there is a runner on third and less than two outs. It's essential to hit the ball far enough into the outfield so that the runner can be tagged and score, even if it means you get out. In a close game, one run can make all the difference.

Smart Base Running: More Than Just Stealing

When you run the bases smart, you help your team score as many runs as possible. Stealing bases is not enough; you must read the game, guess what will happen, and make intelligent basepath choices. Pay attention to how the pitcher throws the ball. Is he getting tired slowly? Is he quick to step up? It can help you choose when to steal and when to throw away a good lead. The number of strikes and balls can affect how you run the bases. When there is a complete count, the pitcher is more likely to focus on the hitter, which gives the runner a chance to steal a base. Running the bases quickly can put pressure on the defenders and make it easier to score. Still, don't be careless. You were learning to weigh the risks and benefits before you try to steal something or take a big lead.

Working Together: The Battery Link

When both the catcher and the baserunner are on the same page, situational hitting and bright base running work best. Talk to your catcher about possible ways to hit and run bases before the game. This lets everyone know what the plan is and how they should act. Catchers talk to baserunners about stealing or taking leads by using minor signs. Set up a clear and regular way to chatter without giving the other side away. To run the bases well, you must believe what the catcher says. Trusting their judgment when they tell you to steal is essential, and you should play the play boldly.

How to Become a Baseball Expert

It takes hard work and a deep understanding of the game to get good at situational hitting and bright base running. When you watch Major League Baseball games, pay close attention to how the pros handle different situations at bat and on the bases. Figure out how they made their choices and use those ideas in your own game. Read books and articles or watch videos online about these techniques. Getting more information can make your skills much better. Situational hitting and base running drills can help you improve your skills and make decisions when stressed. You can practice different situations with your coaches or friends by acting out different game situations.

You can help your team more if you learn how to hit in different situations and run smarter at the plate. You'll be able to score when you have the chance, put pressure on the defense, and help the team win more games. Put on your thinking cap, work on your abilities, and become the player whose skills go beyond hitting and catching. Become the baseball genius your team needs.

A strategic approach

"At the plate."

Entering the batter's box might intimidate hitters. Fastballs, breaking pitches, and pressure to deliver clutter your mind. What if you could become a strategic pilot, piloting the at-bat with a plan and deliberate approach? How to become a hitter who reacts to pitches and sets the terms.

Be aware of your strengths and weaknesses.

Understand your hitting habits before dissecting pitchers. Some self-reflection:

Power vs. Contact: Are you a home run slugger or a contact hitter who puts the ball in play? You can hit pitches for maximum damage or get on base by knowing your strengths.

Stance and Swing: Examine your stance and swing. Are you tall and balanced or crouching? Does your swing have an uppercut or level plane? Understanding your mechanics helps you choose pitches that suit your hitting style.

Hot Zones: Where do you hit the ball most? Do you have gap power and hit the ball anywhere, or are you a pull hitter who favors the outer half of the plate? Knowing this lets you focus on pitches that hit your "hot zones" for consistent contact.

Scouting the Enemy: Pitcher Interpretation

Pregame Scouting Reports describe the pitcher's strengths and flaws. Is he a dominating lefty with a deceptive curveball or a powerful fastball? Does he have trouble controlling or pinpointing pitches? Watch the pitcher's warm-up throws. Look for mechanics inconsistencies that may indicate control difficulties or pitch dependence on the opening pitches of the at-bat matter. See the pitcher's velocity, location, and pitch selection. Starting with this information helps you adapt your at-bat strategy.

Game Planning: Tailoring Your Approach

Be patient against a breaking ball pitcher if you're a fastball batter. Avoid early-count-breaking balls and wait for a fastball you can drive. Does the pitcher struggle with fastball command? Prepare to punish pitches that leak over the plate. Does he overuse his curveball? Adjust your swing for a breaking ball and wait for a fastball later. Avoid one-trick pony. Situationally adapt your strategy. Focus on putting the ball in play and advancing runners early with no outs. Shorten your swing and focus on solid contact for an RBI with runners in scoring position and two strikes. Strategic success requires discipline. Avoid chasing pitches outside the strike zone early in the count. This forces the pitcher to throw strikes and make mistakes you can exploit.

Body Language Cues for Pitcher Storytelling

Robots aren't pitchers. A different windup or lengthier pause before delivery may indicate a curveball pitch. The pitcher's glove position before delivery can reveal the pitch type. One glove may indicate a fastball, while another may indicate a breaking ball. Some pitchers show their emotions through facial expressions, though not always. They may throw a fastball with a frown or an off-speed pitch with a comfortable look.

Mid-Bat Adjustments: Game Adaptation

The best-laid intentions might fail. Analyze your mechanics after each swing. Are you lunging at broken balls? If so, stay back and wait for a manageable fastball. Was the pitcher throwing more sliders after you hit a fastball well? Prepare to swing differently with the new pitch combination. Call a timeout and talk to your coach if you're lost at the plate. Their dugout observations may provide vital insights.

Technology: Data-Driven Decisions

Baseball today uses technology. Your swing mechanics can be evaluated and improved with video analysis. Pitcher habits and location trends can be revealed by pitch data analysis. Data should be used, not ruled. Use facts, intuition, and game-reading to make decisions.

Mental toughness: Focusing Under Pressure

Baseball is mental and physical. Before entering the batter's box, visualize hitting the pitch. Two strikes and a runner on third don't mean disaster. Concentrate on each pitch, breathe deeply, and trust your swing. Everybody strikes out. Do not linger on failures.

Analyze what went wrong, learn from it, and approach the next at-bat positively.

Learning is an ongoing process.

Developing brilliant hitting skills takes a lifetime. Watch Major League Baseball games to see how professional hitters handle different pitchers. Assess their plate discipline and decision-making. Ask expert coaches for assistance or join hitting clinics. These resources offer helpful advice and individualized comments. More live pitching in batting practice or simulated games can help you read pitchers and execute your strategy.

Strategic thinking turns you from a spectator to a pilot in charge of your at-bat. You learn your strengths, vulnerabilities, and how to exploit your opponents'. Hitting requires talent, patience, and strategy. Take on the challenge, trust your intuition, and become the plate-ruler. The pitchers will be frustrated by your effort and practice.

CHAPTER 4

BUILDING STRENGTH AND AGILITY

Tailored workouts

"For catchers"

To be a catcher, you need a particular set of skills. You're in charge of defense, the pitcher trusts you, and you take most of the foul balls. To be great behind the plate, you need a workout plan that is as varied as the things you must do. Here is a step-by-step guide to making a workout plan perfect for a catcher.

The Foundation: Getting more robust and more stable in the core

Think of your core as the most essential part of your ability to catch. You need this for explosive throws, intense squats, and the steadiness to block pitches in the dirt. You must do the basic plank. Hold a high, low, or side plank for extended periods to strengthen your core muscles. The obliques are the muscles on the sides of your core that are important for throwing because they give you spinning power. This one helps keep your core stable so you don't spin when you throw. While keeping your body still, hold a dumbbell in each hand and press it outwards.

Power that explodes: putting heat behind the plate

Catchers aren't just silent receivers but also places where runners can be thrown. These versatile throws work your arm strength and technique by making you throw like a ball. Throwing the medicine ball over your head, sidearm, and even to different bases is possible. Slowly add more weight to the ball you throw to strengthen your arms. Don't give up form to get a heavier ball, work on smooth mechanics with a heavier ball. When you do exercises like box jumps and depth jumps, your legs get more robust and faster, making your throws more powerful.

Lower body strength: holding your throws in place and blocking pitches

All the moves you make behind the plate start with your lower body. Strong legs allow for strong throws, quick sideways moves to catch errant throws, and the ability to take the force of foul balls. Master the lower body with these moves. First, do squats with your body weight, then move on to squats with barbells or dumbbells. Lunges work your quads, hamstrings, and glutes, which are critical for building strength and flexibility in your lower body. The muscles in your back and legs are part of your posterior chain. This exercise strengthens them, which is essential for quick moves like throwing and building power when blocking pitches.

Unleash the Inner Thrower with Rotational Power

A spinning solid core is essential for catchers because it helps them move power from their legs to their throwing arm. To build spinning power, try these exercises: This move strengthens your core and shoulder cuff muscles by making you throw something.

These are like cable chops, but you do them with a medicine ball or something heavy to add speed and explosiveness. Twist your body as you throw the medicine ball to build strength in your core and rotator cuff.

Catching-Specific Drills: Getting Better at the Game

Work on blocking pitches from different angles in the dirt with someone who throws tennis or soft practice balls. Get better at moving your glove slightly to guide pitches into the strike zone. You can use a mirror or a buddy to practice framing. Work on your footwork, throwing techniques, and following through on your throws. Get better at throwing accurately and quickly to different bases.

Flexibility and Mobility: How to Stay Quick Behind the Plate

A catcher needs to be as quick as a cat. When you do mobility and stretching routines regularly, you can avoid injuries and improve your throwing and blocking range of motion. Your legs, hips, shoulders, and core should all be stretched. This is just a plan. Talk to a certified trainer about making a custom plan for your fitness level and goals. Pay attention to your body, rest when needed, and put good form ahead of big weights. It takes hard work and commitment to become a strong and quick catcher. Take your time, enjoy the trip, and remember to celebrate your progress. A well-trained catcher is a strength for any team, especially behind the plate. Put on your cleats and grab your mitt; now you're going to build the body of a great catcher.

Exercises for quickness and agility.

Want your lightning-fast moves to leave defenses in the dust and turn heads? Don't look any further! When it comes to sports and exercise, speed and agility are king. They let you move quickly, change direction quickly, and take control of the field. Here are some workouts that will help you become a master of movement and bring out your inner speed demon.

The Foundation: Making a Strong Base

Ensure your body is ready for the task before doing hard drills. Being quick and agile starts with having a solid core and a stable lower body. To make a strong base, follow these steps:

Variations on the Plank: The standard plank strengthens your core, which is the control center of your body. To work out different core muscles, do high, low, and side planks.

Squats: Master the lower body with these moves. The influential power you need for quick bursts of speed and sharp changes in direction comes from having strong legs.

Lunges: Lunges work your quads, hamstrings, and hips, which are all critical for moving forward and staying balanced when you move quickly.

Step-by-Step Drills for Footwork Finesse

Ladder drills are an essential part of any program for improving agility. These drills help you coordinate your footwork, which lets you move faster and more accurately on the field:

Basic Ladder Drills: Run back and forth over the ladder, landing on each rung with one foot at a time. Slowly make the drills faster and more complex by adding versions like high knees, grapevines, and carioca (sideways shuffle).

Do these agility ladder drills with a partner: Add a person who can throw a tennis ball or ball. Time how long it takes you to do the drill while catching or dodging the ball. This will test your reaction time and hand-eye coordination.

Cone Drills: Get Better at Turns

With cone drills, you can improve your quick and easy direction-changing skills. Arrange the cones differently, like circles, lines, or zigzags. Move quickly from side to side around the cones and keep your center of gravity low. Quickly change direction at each cone and sprint from one to the next. It makes you stronger and faster by making you do this drill. Backpedal around the cones while keeping your eyes forward and your body low. This makes it easier to run away and adapt to new conditions quickly.

Plyometric Exercises: Make Your Moves Stronger

Plyometric workouts use short bursts of strength to help you move quickly like you need to do in sports. For faster starts, jumps, and changes of direction, these drills help you build up powerful force:

"Box Jumps": Jump on a stable box and fall gently. As your explosiveness gets better, slowly raise the box higher.

Depth Jumps: Step off a platform (carefully!), jump down, and then jump back up quickly. This practice strengthens your legs and teaches you how to handle impact properly.

Squat Jumps: Squat down and then jump straight up quickly. This exercise makes your legs and core more vital, which lets you move faster.

Reactive Drills: Get Your Reflexes Ready

Quickness isn't just moving quickly; it also means responding rapidly to things around you. These drills will help you improve your reflexes:

Ball Drops: Have a person drop a ball in front of you no matter what. As fast as you can, either catch it or jump over it. When you do partner hand slaps, stand facing your partner and randomly slap each other's hands. This drill helps you respond faster and coordinate your hands and eyes better.

Mirror Drills: Turn your back to a mirror and move around while copying your image as quickly as possible. This helps you focus on good form and improves your balance and reaction time at the same time.

Start slowly and pay attention to your form. As you get better, make the drills harder and more complicated. Do what your body tells you, take days off, and prioritize avoiding injuries. Defenders will be left in your wake as you show off your improved speed and agility on the field if you work hard and get the proper training.

Focusing on leg strength

"And endurance"

Legs that are strong and flexible are essential for all athletes. They move you forward, keep you stable for quick moves, and help you through long workouts. Getting more robust and durable legs is essential whether you're a runner, a bodybuilder, or just someone who wants to go up and down stairs without any problems. Here's how to make legs that you'll be proud of.

The Strength Squad: Building a Strong Base

Leg strength is essential for solid movements, quick starts, and lifting big things, and it is, without a doubt, the best workout for your lower body. Your legs, hamstrings, glutes, and calves are just a few of the muscle groups that squats work. First, do squats with your body weight, then move on to squats with barbells or dumbbells. Make sure you use the proper form to maximize your workout and avoid getting hurt. Lunges are a great way to work out specific leg muscles and improve balance. You can use your body weight, dumbbells, or a hammer to do them. To work out different muscle groups, try walking lunges, reverse lunges, and Bulgarian split squats, all variations on the lunge. Deadlifts work your posterior chain, which comprises muscles in your back and legs. These muscles are essential for decisive actions like sprinting and jumping. Start with smaller weights until you get the form right. Then, add more weight.

Getting Stronger: Legs That Won't Give Out

It's great to have strong legs, but they need to be able to keep going. Running is an easy way to build leg strength that works well. Start by going for short lengths at a steady pace. Slowly add more distance and speed to your workouts as you get fitter. You might try interval training to boost your endurance, which involves going back and forth between short bursts of high intensity and rest times. A great way to test your legs and build endurance is to run uphill. Find a hill with a modest grade, run up it quickly, and then jog back down to rest. Do this cycle a certain number of times. As you get stronger, make the hill farther away or steeper. Climbing stairs is an easy and effective way to make your legs stronger. Find a steep set of stairs and slowly go up them. If you want to make it harder, you can jump two steps at a time or wear weights in your backpack.

A Multifaceted Approach to Circuit Training

Circuit training is a challenging workout that includes strength and endurance exercises. This method makes your legs work in new ways, keeps your heart rate up, and burns calories. Here is an example of a circuit:

- Ten squats
- 15 lunges on each leg
- 30 seconds on the wall
- 1 minute of jumping jacks

Do this cycle one after the other for a set number of rounds, taking short breaks between sets. As your fitness level rises, you can keep pushing yourself by adding more reps, rounds, or rest time.

Don't Forget the Extra Cast: Glutes and Calves

You need to have strong legs and glutes to avoid injuries and perform at your best. You can do these with your body weight, dumbbells, or a machine. Pay attention to how slowly and carefully you lift and lower your feet. Lay on your back with your feet flat on the floor and your knees bent. Squeeze your glutes as you lift your hips off the ground. Don't let go until you've held for a few seconds.

Fire Up Your Engine: Nutrition and Rest

You need to eat right and rest to build solid and long-lasting legs. Ensure you're getting enough protein in your food to help your muscles grow and heal. Also, don't skimp on carbs because they give you energy for your workouts. Rest and healing should come first after a hard workout. You need to stretch every day to get more flexible and keep your muscles from getting sore. You might want to use a foam roller to work out tight muscles and get more blood flowing.

Listen to Your Body: How to Avoid Overtraining

It's good to push yourself, but paying attention to your body is also essential. Take a day off if you are in pain. If you train too much, you could hurt yourself and have to take time off. Always being the same is essential. If you train regularly and ensure you heal correctly, you will see better results than if you only do intense workouts sometimes.

You can build legs of steel if you work hard and do a range of exercises. This plan will help you get where you want to go, whether you want explosive power, steady endurance, or a mix of the two. Get ready to crush those workouts, leave your limits behind, and enjoy the feeling of having strong, flexible legs.

THE LEADER ON THE FIELD

Embracing your role

"As the team's on-field leader"

When you step behind the plate, you do more than catch throws. It means being the face of peace for your pitcher, the leader on the field, and the quarterback of the defense. For this job, you need more than just physical strength. You also need to be smart, communicate well, and have a lot of heart. Here's how to step up as a leader and become the rock that your team looks to:

Be an Idea Leader, not a Tyrant

Giving directions is not being a leader. Knowing the game, the other team, and, most importantly, your player is essential. Read scouting reports and look at how hitters usually hit, then use what you've learned to call pitches carefully. But talking to each other is essential. Talk to your pitcher about your plan, listen to what they say, and work with them to make the perfect strike zone.

Building a solid foundation of confidence

The act of pitching can be nerve-wracking. Worse things can happen after one bad pitch. You are the catcher, so it's your job to be the pitcher's biggest fan. Give them words of support after a tough out, a pat on the back after a strikeout, and your presence when things are stressful. Telling your pitcher you believe in them will boost their confidence, leading to great throwing.

Set a good example

Things you do say louder than words. Take the time to learn the game, and always try to improve. Don't be lazy in practice or on the field. Be the first person to help a friend who has made a mistake. Your teammates will be motivated by your hard work and determination and will see you as a leader they can look up to and follow.

Make your messages clear.

A strong team depends on being able to talk to each other. You can confidently call pitches using short, clear signs that the pitcher can understand immediately. Do not be afraid to tell your coaches or friends what you think if something is wrong. A good leader will speak up if needed, but they will do so with respect and the team's success in mind.

Take the Pressure

To be the leader on the field, you have to be able to handle the pressure. Sometimes, the result depends on your decision, close games, and tough calls. Don't be afraid of these times; enjoy them. Lead your team through good times and bad. Keep in mind that real leaders shine best when things are at stake.

If you embrace these traits, you'll go from being a player to a real leader. A natural leader builds trends and plans and leaves everything on the field to win.

Communicating effectively

"With coaches and teammates."

Being the catcher isn't just about having the right gear and being tough; it's also about being the defense's primary point of contact. You connect the player on the mound to the rest of the team. How to improve your conversation and get everyone on the same page:

How to Get Your Pitcher to Trust You

Your thrower is a partner in crime. From the start, set up a straightforward way to communicate. Talk about the best signs to use for each pitch, and make sure you practice them often. Build relationships beyond the rules. As you call pitches, talk to your starter about what they do well and what they could do better. Build trust so they can voice worries or suggest different pitches without fear of being judged.

Talk to people clearly and concisely.

Don't bother with secret handshakes and codes. Use constant, clear signs that your pitcher can understand immediately, especially when things are. If you think your player is doing something wrong or if you have a strong feeling about a particular pitch, speak up. Don't be afraid to say what you think, but be polite and keep your pitcher's success in mind.

Master the art of communicating without words.

Body language says a lot. After a close pitch, a raised eyebrow can let your players know they need to make changes. A quick nod and a smile can help someone feel better. Communicate with your players through your body language and help them stay focused during the game.

Work as a Team, Not Alone

It is not only you and the player who can talk to each other. Give your friends helpful information. Tell the outfielders that a batter likes to pull the ball, or let the infield know that someone might be trying to steal. Your teammates will be better able to make plays if they have more knowledge.

Talk to your coaches openly.

On the field, the teachers show you the way. Don't be afraid to ask them for help during breaks or pitch changes. If there is an apparent weakness in the batter's method, suggest a way to take advantage of it. Talking to coaches freely helps everyone work together to make a good plan.

Communication works best when it goes both ways. Listen carefully, follow your coaches' directions, and be open to what your teammates have to say. Encouraging open conversation and trust will strengthen the group so everyone works together to finish the mission.

Setting a positive example

"And maintaining a strong work ethic."

You're in charge as a catcher, not just behind home plate. The people on your team watch every move you make and every mood you show. How to be a good leader and have a strong work attitude that motivates your team to do their best:

Be the Machine of Hard Work

Do not give up on a play. Do not stop trying to catch poor throws. Do an entire run after each throw. Your drive is inspiring. Seeing you do it makes your friends want to give it their all. Every out-and-play deserves your best effort; the whole team does better when you do that.

Keep a positive attitude.

Being positive is strong. Bad calls and dropped strikes happen all the time. Do not think about them too much. Instead of getting angry, smile, say something nice to your pitcher, or give a partner a high five. Your good mood sets the tone for the whole team. This makes a helpful setting where mistakes are seen as chances to learn rather than reasons to give up.

Learn how to play the game.

Knowledge is indeed power. Show that you care about the team by learning new things and improving constantly. Learn from scouting reports, game films, and teachers or experienced players willing to give you advice. Your commitment to continually learning shows how serious you are about the game and motivates your friends to similarly work on getting better.

Take responsibility

No one is perfect. Take responsibility for your mistakes. If a dropped ball leads to a run, apologize to your pitcher or friends. Take what you've learned and move on. Being accountable for your actions builds trust within the group and shows that you want the group to succeed.

Fight for your teammates.

Help your friends feel better. Honor their wins, no matter how big or small. Reward them with a pat on the back after a great catch or a fist bump after a big K. Thanks for your help. It creates a sense of community where everyone feels valued and wants to participate.

You don't have to bark directions to be a leader; you must set a good example. You can motivate your coworkers to reach their full potential with a solid work ethic, a positive attitude, and a commitment to continually improving. On and off the field, your guidance will be the key to building a strong, united team that loves competing for wins.

CHAPTER 6

Staying Sharp and Focused

Developing mental toughness

"And resilience"

Physical and mental strength must be just right to be a catcher. A frustrated pitcher, a hungry attack, and the constant attention of the game all put pressure on you. Don't worry, player! Mind toughness and perseverance can be improved, just like any other skill. Here are some ways to improve your mental game and become a strong force behind the plate:

Take a ride on the roller coaster:

There are highs and lows in baseball. Don't judge your work by a passed ball or a stolen base. Accept that the game will go up and down over time. Pay attention to the next pitch and forget about the mistakes you've made. Mental toughness means getting back on your feet quickly, learning from mistakes, and keeping your mind on the job at hand.

See yourself succeeding

The mind is vital. Before each game, close your eyes and picture yourself doing a great job. Think about how you would frame pitches perfectly, call the right ones for strikeouts, and lead your team to win. Visualization makes you feel more sure of yourself and trains your mind to expect success, which increases the chances that it will happen.

Fight off negative thoughts.

Sometimes, the noise in your head is the worst thing that can happen to you. When negative thoughts like "I can't catch this fastball" or "We're going to lose" come up, say something positive to fight them: your skills and the things you've done well in the past. Pay attention to the things you can change: how hard you work, feel, and talk to people.

"Learn from Your Mistakes"

Everybody messes up sometimes. The important thing is to move on from them and learn from them. Think about what went wrong after the game, but don't be hard on yourself. Use your mistakes to help you get better. Talk to your teachers for feedback and devise ways to prevent this from happening again.

Take the Pressure

Pressure is a good thing. It means that your part is essential and can significantly affect how the game turns out. Don't run away from stress; learn how to do well. Learn ways to relax, like deep breathing or meditation, to help you stay calm and focused when things get tough. Remember that pressure can be your fuel, pushing you to do your best.

Get help from your support system.

Mental toughness doesn't just happen on its own. Get help from your family, coaches, and friends. It's essential to surround yourself with people who believe in you and discuss your problems. A robust support system gives you hope, push, and a safe place to deal with the ups and downs of the game.

By building mental toughness and resilience, you can take charge of your feelings instead of letting them control you. Behind the plate, you become unshakeable, a leader who builds trust, and a player who does well under pressure. A mentally tough catcher can change the game; your mind is the key to reaching your full ability. You can do it. Take a deep breath, believe in yourself, and prepare to face the mental obstacles and come out on top.

Strategies for staying engaged

"During long games"

Baseball games can be long, complex tests of your mental and physical strength. As a catcher, staying interested during a long game is essential. Now that rounds seem to go on forever, here are some ways to keep your mind sharp and your energy up:

Feed Your Body

Baseball is a sport for smart people, but it also tests your physical strength. Bring healthy food like nuts, fruits, or granola bars to keep your energy up during the game. Remember to drink water—it's your best friend. Stay hydrated during the game to keep your mind clear and avoid getting tired.

Mind Breaks

Everyone needs a break every once in a while. Find ways to take your mind off of the game in between sets. Talk to your friends briefly, do light stretches, or even close your eyes and take a few deep breaths. These short breaks help you get your mind back on the game to start the next inning feeling ready to do well.

Have Fun

Let's be honest: baseball can get old. In the long run, find ways to make things more fun. Enjoy the fans' antics, joke with your friends, or play a quick game of "I Spy" in your head with something in the outfield. These little moments of fun can help you stay happy and upbeat.

Stay hydrated and cool.

Being too hot or thirsty makes it hard to concentrate. Keep calm and drink plenty of water, especially during long summer games. Regularly wear sunscreen, wear a hat letting air pass through, and cool off your face and neck with a damp towel between games. Being comfortable enables you to focus on the game instead of what's bothering you outside of it.

See yourself succeeding

Visualizing things is a handy skill. Close your eyes during breaks or pitch changes and picture yourself correctly framing pitches, calling the correct pitches for strikeouts, and leading your team to victory. This mental practice helps you stay focused on the game and keep a good attitude.

Be in the Present Moment

Thinking about mistakes you've made in the past or moves you want to make in the future takes your mind off of the present. Pay attention to the job: catching the next pitch, talking to your pitcher, and planning how to help the batter. Being in the present moment lets you act naturally and do your best.

Help Your Teammates

Everyone can get tired after a long game. Spread good vibes to your friends. Encourage them, enjoy their wins, and keep an attitude of working as a team. Your good mood can spread to the rest of the team and keep them inspired and interested.

Staying interested in a long game takes a run, not a sprint. Using these tips, you'll stay focused, save energy, and stay an essential part of your team, ready to lead them to win no matter how many innings it takes.

Recovery, nutrition, and maintaining

"Peak physical condition"

On the field, being a catcher is like being a warrior. You get struck by foul balls, squat for many pitches, and use up much energy running the game. To stay at your best and avoid getting hurt, you must focus on healing, nutrition, and staying in top physical shape. Here's how to make your body a well-tuned machine for catching:

Recovery rituals include time to rest, relax, and fix things.

The time when your body gets stronger is not when you work out but when you heal. Put sleep first! Try to get 7-8 hours of sound sleep each night so your muscles can recover, and your mind can rest. Stretching after a game is very important. Hold light stretches for each major muscle group to keep them from getting sore and to make them more flexible. You might want to use a foam roller to work out tight muscles and get more blood flowing.

"Fire Up Your Machine: Eating for Performance"

Food keeps you going. A well-balanced diet with lots of complex carbs for long-lasting energy, lean protein for building and repairing muscles, and healthy fats for brain health is what you should eat. Don't skimp on fruits and veggies if you want enough vitamins and minerals. Meals before a game should be light but give you energy that lasts. For example, a chicken breast sandwich on whole-wheat bread or oats with berries. Meals after a game should focus on mending muscle tissue and restocking glycogen stores. Grilled fish with brown rice and roasted vegetables is what you should order.

Water is vital.

Picture your body as a car. It gets too hot and breaks down without the proper cooling (water!). Drink plenty of water all day, before, during, and after games. Carry a water bottle you can use repeatedly, and drink from it often, even if you're not thirsty. Staying hydrated helps you focus, keeps you from getting tired, and makes your body work at its best.

Pay attention to your body.

It's good to push yourself, but paying attention to your body is also essential. If you have pain that won't go away, don't ignore it. Take a day off or change how you work out. If you try to push through pain, you could hurt yourself badly and be out of action for a long time.

Strength Training: Keeping Your Fortress Strong

Don't forget to do strength exercises! You will stay physically strong behind the plate if you do routines that work on your core, leg power, and upper body strength regularly. You might want to work with a trainer to make a custom plan that targets your weaknesses and meets your needs.

Take a listen to the experts.

There's no shame in getting help from a professional. A sports nutritionist can help you improve your ability by making a personalized meal plan. A physical therapist can look at how your body moves and offer exercises to keep you from getting hurt. These experts can help you achieve your goal of being in the best shape possible.

You become an unstoppable force behind the plate if you put healing first, feed your body well, and stay in great shape. A well-fed and rested catcher is ready to take over the game!

Closing Thoughts

As we end this trip, I hope you feel ready to take the field with confidence. There's more to being a catcher than just getting the ball. You'll learn how to be a leader, a planner, and the defense key for your team. These drills and techniques are just the beginning. Try different things until you find the best one and create your own style. Enjoy the tasks, be happy about the wins, and most of all, have fun! Baseball is a game, and catching should be a fun way to learn about yourself and grow. There is always more to learn for the best catches. Always try to improve, study the game more, and ask teachers and mentors for help. You're well on your way to becoming a great catcher who inspires confidence, leads by example, and rules the game with your hard work, passion, and the knowledge you've learned here. Take your stuff to the field, and let's hear that "play ball!"